girls'
guide to
diy

Girls' Guide to DIY

by Salli Brand

Dave Brand, my lovely, lovely Dad. This is for you.

First published in Great Britain in 2004
by Mitchell Beazley, an imprint of
Octopus Publishing Group Limited,
2–4 Heron Quays, London E14 4JP
© Octopus Publishing Group Limited 2004

All rights reserved. No part of this publication may be reproduced
or utilized in any form by any means, electronic or mechanical,
including photocopying, recording, or by any information storage
and retrieval system, without prior written permission of the publisher.

ISBN 1 84533 015 3

A CIP catalogue record for this book is available from the British Library.

While all reasonable care has been taken during the preparation of
this edition, neither the publisher, editors, nor the author can accept
responsibility for any consequences arising from the use thereof
or from the information contained therein.

Senior Executive Editor **Anna Sanderson**
Executive Art Editor **Auberon Hedgecoe**
Illustrator **Yadzia Williams**
Senior Editor **Emily Anderson**
Design **Colin Goody**
Production **Seyhan Esen**
Copy Editor **Colette Campbell**
Proofreader **Barbara Mellor**

Set in Gill Sans Light, Loki Cola, Magda, Calvert and Swiss

To order this book as a gift or an incentive
contact Mitchell Beazley on 020 7531 8481

Printed and bound by Mackays Ltd, UK

MITCHELL BEAZLEY

girls'
guide to
diy

Salli
Brand

contents

introduction

When I grow up I think I'm going to be one of those plate-spinners you sometimes see in variety shows. You know the ones: 24 plates spinning wildly on top of long sticks and just as soon as one starts to wobble the chap gives the stick a few turns and none of them ever comes crashing down. I'd be a great plate-spinner, I'm sure, because (as for most women) multi-tasking and coping abilities have arrived in my life by default. Work, college, dog, personal appearance, time to relax, time to eat … and then along comes the home on a budget with all its quirks and leaks and things to be done. And oh, yes, time to enjoy a relationship?

This book is for you if you need a bit of really basic information on how to cope with day-to-day household improvements and minor disasters. It's for you if you have little time for your home but big dreams for it. A book for the busy girl with no time or money for someone else to come in and cope for you.

Now if you see yourself as a DIY aficionado, and already own your own pipe bender and skill saw, you may be too advanced to need this little book, and there are plenty of very detailed help books for those of us who really get the bug. However, nothing is as good a tutor as personal experience; this book is at the "how to boil an egg" end of the DIY spectrum, without having to ask your Dad!

research the neighbourhood

If you are moving to a new home, or have plans to renovate and redecorate your existing house, you may start to have imaginary baths in the new bathroom, imaginary dinner parties in the new improved kitchen, and in your mind it's the perfect sanctuary.

Time to do a reality check then. The truth will of course be quite different, but you don't need me to tell you that. I bet you're not doing imaginary decorating are you? So stop daydreaming, because there are loads of things you can do before you get you started on the hard graft.

find your local trade paint supplier

You will thank me for this in time. Trade paint dries in half the time it takes for normal paint to dry, it covers in fewer coats, costs heaps less and comes complete with a friendly bloke behind the counter who knows everything about paint and decorating.

● trade paint dries in half the time of normal paint

Top all that with the fact that your local supplier will be pleased to do business with you and always has a shop full of fit painter-decorators who are a genuinely friendly breed, and you'll never buy painting supplies from a DIY shop again.

find the local dump

Commit the opening hours to memory; you will be spending
a lot of time here. Do they take empty chocolate boxes,
take-away wrappings, and wine bottles too?

find the plumbing supply centre

You might not think you need any plumbing stuff yet, but this
place could save your life if you get unexpected leaks. They
know all the local plumbers too, so ask for recommendations –
better than taking a gamble with the local telephone directory.

find the local electrical wholesaler

A light-switch cover costs quite a bit from my nearest big DIY
store down the road. The one I bought was a quarter of that
price, from charming, friendly Andy at the electrical wholesaler in
the little town centre. He even told me how to fit it. Electricians
are far and away the brightest (ha!) of the tradesmen.

sign up with a mail-order DIY supplier

There are a couple of these out there. They're cheap, good
quality, and they deliver to you the next day if your order is more
than a certain amount, wherever you are. They'll even deliver to

your office. You can get their names by stopping for a chat
in the street with any good-looking tradesman. What a bonus.

buy a good-quality, safe pair of steps

Please.

find out exactly where the nearest accident and emergency facility is

Find out where the car park and main entrance are and commit
the route to memory. You think it will never happen but it could.

find the nearest big weekend market

One of those that set up on an old airfield-type space, rather than
a cutesy village market. Don't expect to find top of the range
unless it's end-of-line stock, but markets are superb for your
temporary homemaking bits while you save up for the real thing.

and finally the natives

Check out your neighbours and any unwritten parking rules. Who
parks in that space right outside, which you would like to use
when you need to unload a car full of heavy items? Who drives
any commercial vehicles? Could be a gorgeous electrician!

choose a style

Every home, particularly if it isn't a brand-new build, will almost
certainly have a kind of style already. Whether or not you like
it is quite another question. Keeping the existing style and
decoration is an option of course, but there is a danger that
you could get used to it and still be staring up at flouncy
lampshades three years down the line. Take my Dad: he
bought a house with lurid wallpaper in the hallway yonks
ago. It was probably expensive stuff but it was horrible.
Well, the wallpaper finally came down last year and that
was only because the brickwork needed some major repairs.
The house is now transformed! So beware – if you decide to
live with something for a while you might end up putting up
with it for longer than you anticipated.

● give yourself a blank canvas on which to work your style magic

The best way forward is to give yourself a blank canvas on
which to work your style magic. Take everything out and paint
the room white or a neutral colour. In this way you will be able
to see how your own favourite things can fit in. And you'll get
an idea of how to build some style around them. Putting all
your bits and bobs in the attic and bringing them down when

you have a real place for them is not a bad way to start.
You'll be amazed at how much never comes down again.

● choose a single item as your style inspiration

One of the golden rules of interior design is to let the customer
suggest a starting point. It might be the sofa or even just a
postcard they have kept because they like the picture. You
probably have one or two favourite things, or maybe an
inspirational picture from a magazine. Let this be your first
building block.

Style is a funny word; it smacks of class and conformity.
In truth there are no rules and you can go your own sweet
way without having to stick to any rigid confines. Now who
would ever decide on a style inspired by a beautiful Italian
pepper mill? If the only thing you have that you really love
to look at is the world's finest pepper grinder and you
want to show it off, then what better place to begin to start
creating your environment? And the house is coming along
very nicely, I'll have you know.

have vision

This is where we all become management gurus for a while. The vision of how your home will be is the driving force for getting you out of bed on a Saturday morning and up that new ladder.

If you change the old decor to something plain and neutral you will be able to sit down with a glass of wine and stare at the blank walls and dream. A shoebox of photographs from magazines; pictures of the fireplace you want but can't afford; a dream coffee table that you've never actually seen but know you want. Visualize how it will actually be when, one day, it is finished. Writing lists will stoke the fires of your imagination. Having a surge of enthusiasm is so exciting, and it's amazing how focused it can make you.

● don't waste money on second best

Now this is really important if you want to avoid doing everything twice. When you come up with a mind's-eye picture of how the place will look, make it the real picture and not a budget half-way house based on your current circumstances. I have wasted so much time and money on making do with second best – I realized recently that student habits die hard. I am a grown woman now, and even worse in my case is the fact

that I make my living bringing other people's dreams to life – properly. So what am I doing up this ladder with a staple gun?

My original vision is still there, pretty much unchanged, but like a fool I am now throwing out my short-cut purchases as the better stuff begins to filter in. When I did some quick sums of how much I had spent on temporary items of furniture, vases, teacups, and styling, before sticking to my own golden rule, I was horrified.

And that golden rule is? Have little but have good. Minimalism is a style. Minimalism as a style is a brilliant way of disguising the fact that you haven't yet actually got anything decent to put in your home.

● the golden rule?
have little but have good

So, picture how you want it to be, from a tap that no longer drips right up to the new bed on a beautiful floor. Hang in there with the vision. Work as slowly as you need. Take no prisoners and make as few compromises as you can. Cut those acrylic fingernails a bit shorter – you can have them back anytime you want. Put on your overalls and let's get started.

buy, hire, or borrow?

You could easily spend a fortune buying tools and DIY kit that you won't use that often. As someone who hates "stuff" that takes up valuable storage space, I bear in mind the size of an item when deciding whether to buy it. A wallpaper stripper for example – just too huge to consider having one of those to keep. A jig-saw, on the other hand, is useful for chopping up kindling wood, cutting curves and straights in all sorts of bits of wood and metal, and is used almost as much as the iron.

buying

The best piece of advice I ever received on the subject of buying tools was: "buy the best quality you can afford but consider how much each use will cost". Easy, like working out the cost-per-wear of a coveted jacket or pair of designer trousers.

> ● **buy the best quality you can afford but consider how much each use will cost**

A really cheap tool may not last a single weekend, so be warned about paying too little. You can usually tell the quality of a tool by looking at the metalwork and handles. There's something about the really dodgy ones that looks cheap; the metal is more matt than shiny and the plastic of the handles looks brittle. Quality is

"don't buy second-hand cast-offs"

a subtle distinction, but a look along the shelves of any tool shop will show you the difference. With power tools your safety is of paramount importance, so don't go buying second-hand cast-offs; stick to well-known brands that have a one-year guarantee.

hiring

Hiring is great – it is a cheap way of gaining access to a specific tool. On average, hiring for 24 hours costs about five per cent of the price of buying the item, depending on size. One of the big benefits is the fact that in good hire shops every tool has a thorough test of the electrics before each loan. You know for sure that the tool you are using is correctly wired and connected.

borrowing

If you borrow a tool you can bet that it will wear out or break down when you have got it. It might have been used a hundred times before with no problems but it won't work at your house. Trust me on this. Avoid borrowing tools at any cost, even from your Dad. If anyone wants to help you by lending you a tool then get them to come around and do the necessary work with it. Another reason for not buying too many of your own tools: if you don't own one then nobody can borrow it and bring it back broken!

plan your time

Some jobs demand to be done in double-quick time, and others can be done at a more leisurely pace. Obviously the unexpected, such as leaks and dead fuses, will require immediate attention.

With work that you choose to do it's a different story, and you'll be surprised at how much you can get done in a day when you are truly motivated. Set yourself a target to achieve before you stop work. It might be to complete a section of the work or to use up a whole tin of paint.

Either way try not to overstretch yourself, because this results in rushed and shoddy work. Having too much in your sights for the day's work can also mean you rush to the point of being a danger to yourself. I've made a few visits to the hospital with cuts no plaster can fix, and I can assure you that each one was the result of a momentary lack of concentration or of tiredness.

My worst accident was working overnight, having worked all day, just to meet a deadline. Three hours in casualty and three days off work later, the job was even more delayed than it would have been had I gone home to bed. The same applies to any tradesmen you are paying. They need sleep too.

essential kit

It is really liberating for a girl to have her own tool kit – matching and co-ordinating tools are cool. Love it! There are some things you must have, so get these on your Christmas list; the rest you can buy as you discover your special requirements.

- Set of various screwdrivers, including the tiny ones
- A small ball pein hammer (ball-backed instead of claw)
- A medium claw hammer
- One or two cheap chisels (to use as jemmies and wedges)
- Long-nosed pliers, Ordinary pliers
- Small hacksaw (junior hacksaw), Basic wood saw
- Mole grips (vital, can't live without them)
- Drill (a hand drill is enough to start with)
- Side cutters (these are like little pliers but with a cutting edge)
- A few sheets of sandpaper
- A pot of super-fast-drying filler
- A flexible filler knife.
- A mastic gun and two inserts, for mastic and strong glue
  - Adjustable spanner
    - A selection of decent-quality screws and nails, small and medium
      - Hip and trendy tool box or bag

22

when to call in the professionals

There are times when coping by yourself just isn't going to work, and you will at some point need expert help. Most often the point at which you will call in a professional is when you reach the limits of your knowledge or of your understanding of a situation. Sometimes you will need a professional because he or she has the specialist tools and knows how to use them.

Watch and learn! Just like watching someone do your nails, you quickly learn how to do them for yourself. The first leaking valve you get on a radiator is hopefully the last time you'll need to call out a plumber to fix it.

"watch and learn"

Follow all the common-sense avenues first, but as soon as you find yourself on unfamiliar territory consider this: if you carry on by yourself, is it only a nuisance job that you hate doing, or is there a safety issue? Are you capable and confident? If the answer is no, then now is the time to introduce yourself to one of your local tradespeople.

When the washing machine wouldn't start until I kicked the door shut, it was obvious that some message was not getting through from the door closing to the motor. A quick look inside the lid with the plug out showed me a sort of switch thingy by the door catch. So I took it out carefully and went out for a replacement. Easy and obvious. I was chuffed to bits at fixing it, too. Now the dishwasher is making a dreadful noise like it has nuts and bolts in it. I've had a look and can't easily get to any of the bits; the screws are ones for professionals, not mere mortals like us. Actually I have one of those professional screwdrivers and I'm studying electrics right now, but I'm not so daft as to dabble in a wet dishwasher. This is where I draw the line. Ho hum, I have to get a little man in.

"your gender doesn't matter, if it's

Use your head. Professionals are trained and have plenty of practice. On the whole they're a nice bunch of good earthy people, too. Is it really worth the money saved to attempt something that may be beyond you? Being alive is quite nice, so get help just before you reach your limit.

know your
limitations

It is a great honour to be born female. I really, really, believe this and being a woman isn't going to stop me from doing things that are considered traditionally male jobs or pastimes. If that is what I want to do, and if I can cope. Welding for example: who said only men can weld? (Think *Flashdance*!)

Physical strength is an issue, of course, but beyond that nothing should hold us back. You don't have to surrender your femininity either. There is a balance between doing physical (and often mucky) work and being as ladylike as ever you were before you took the project on. Sure, you'll find yourself in the DIY shops covered in dust and paint, but that's nothing to be ashamed of.

what you want to do then do it"

There are people out there who subscribe to the view that all women who work or hobby in a physical and male-dominated environment are tough and masculine. Either that or they are trying to prove a point about equality. Not true. The female electrician with whom I worked on an otherwise totally male

25

building site, is very pretty and quiet-natured and good at her job. We can never stop being female in terms of how we absorb comments and dwell on them. Indeed, she and I cried together in the ladies one afternoon, all over our hard hats and bright yellow jackets, because we were both having a hard time of it there. But it didn't take long for us to be back on form, and no one else knew about that. Being in a male-dominated world is fun. Male company is vibrant, challenging, and interesting. Gender doesn't matter; if it's what you want to do then do it.

● shortcuts and tricks of the trade come only with experience

You will always meet people who find you a bit quirky because you are working on your house yourself, but in general you will be admired for your results regardless of being male or female. Women may work more slowly than men, but we do take time out to read the instructions! We tend to be more methodical and perhaps don't take quite so many shortcuts or use tricks of the trade to achieve the same results. These shortcuts come only with experience and through conversations with other people in the know.

"paint ceilings to tone-up before

You will work out for yourself where your limitations lie and hopefully be sensible enough to draw the line at this stage. There are some obvious areas where you might reach a point where you have to stop and reconsider how best to complete a task before carrying on.

muscle power

Cherish your back: you only get one. It is a fact, non-negotiable, that most women are physically less strong than most men. It is also a fact that people who regularly exercise certain muscle groups will be stronger in that area. Spend a week or two painting ceilings with a brush and all of those lovely muscles in your back will develop along with your upper arms. Paint ceilings for the weeks just before you go to a strapless-dress do! Paint a ceiling for a day having had no practice, and you are going to know about it in aches and pains the next day.

● build strength and tone by doing a DIY workout

If body toning is something you would like to achieve alongside the results of your labours, then treat your DIY work as

you go to a strapless-dress do!"

seriously as a workout in the gym, because you will build strength and tone by doing DIY:

- Carry heavy paint tins and bags slightly higher than you would normally: great for the biceps.
- Stand firm and straight, don't sit, and balance the bulk of your weight alternately on each leg rather than just on the stronger one: great for the calves.
- If you do something that really taxes your muscles, a good-quality pure protein shake within 45 minutes of ending for the day encourages muscle repair and definition without putting on the fat that carbohydrates can bring. Get one from a health food shop with pre-digested protein and amino acids.

As I am one of the world's little people, you would not expect me to be able to lift and carry much. However, I took a fitness test a while back and was staggered to find that I am 75 per cent stronger than the norm for a woman of my size and build. This has come from having a physical job.

There are statutory limitations on how heavy a weight one person can lift when working. Normally a single sack of a heavy product, such as sand or cement mix, is the limit, so stick to one at a time. Lifting too much can cause accidents. If you can't comfortably carry something, stop and get help.

multi-tasking

I fail to understand why it is, but we women always seem to have more than one pressing project on the go at any one time. What this means is that we are less able to apply ourselves to our DIY for a whole stretch of time, such as an entire weekend. I've given up trying, and now set myself much more realistic targets. My house comes along more slowly than my men friends' houses, but I also get things done in the rest of my life.

I've a little trick that means that I can live with an unfinished job quite happily for a period of time. At the end of a working day, say spent taking down old cornices or stripping off old wallpaper, I allow an hour to run over the whole lot, lumps, bumps, and dirty marks, with a roller and cheap white paint. This gives a nice clean surface to live with until I next get back to the job and is less depressing than that kind of scruffy building-site look. Of course you can set yourself smaller tasks when time is short, but at some point you'll have to do something that can't be finished in one hit. I can't live in a mess. You might be able to put up with it, but the white-paint ruse works for me and makes me feel less pressured to finish, so other things get some time spent on them too.

technical know-how

This is not just a girl thing; if you don't understand what needs to be done and how, then you are shoulder to shoulder with another limitation. Don't quit at this stage though, not until you are sure you can't go on. Take some advice from the professionals, for example the local paint centre or plumbing store. This is adding to your all-round knowledge, and next time it comes up you will know what to do. Be careful of really alien territory though, like electrics or fixing the guttering. Never be ashamed to admit that you have reached the limit of your knowledge or capabilities. Fixing it after you've made a hash of the job might make it worse than it was before you started.

"careful of electrics or complex jobs"

decorating

preparation

Decoration is only skin deep, and the mantra to remember is "it's only paint!". It doesn't matter if you make a bad first colour choice – once all the preparation and making good of a room has been done then you won't have to do it all over again just to change the colour. The topcoat, be it paint or wallpaper, is probably the quickest and most fun bit of decorating a room.

Preparation is the key word, and the horrid bit. Think in terms of spending two-thirds or more of your time preparing and you'll be about in the ball park. What you need to aim for in preparing to paint or paper is smoothness:

- Sandpaper absolutely everything, yes, even the walls that look OK will be grateful for a quick whizz all over with a medium-grade sandpaper.

- Fill any unwanted holes, such as where shelves used to be or pictures hung. Look for filler that is sandable. Lots of the ready-mixed ones are not and they might dry as rock-solid lumps. Try the white powder filler that you mix up for yourself in small quantities.

• aim for smoothness when preparing to paint or paper

"it's only paint!"

- Fill holes using a flexible filler knife or a bendy piece of smooth plastic. Overfill slightly and leave it to dry. Then you can simply sandpaper the filler smooth against the wall.

- For really big holes there is expandable foam filler, where all you have to do is dampen the edges of the hole and squirt. Watch out because it expands like mad. When it is dry you can cut away the excess and fill the top with sandable filler just like a smaller hole.

- Take down the curtain pole and loosen up the plug sockets so that you can paint behind them. It does make a difference to the end results.

- If existing wallpaper is sound, you need not strip it – just paint over it as if it was plain lining paper.

"paint with the consistency of

painting

A good painted finish takes practice and experience, but here are some really helpful tricks that will give you at least two years' of experience headstart:

thin your paint!

When paint comes out of the can it is usually thick like clotted cream and will cover thickly and quickly. But it will leave brush marks all over the place and that little square where you run carefully around a plug socket is going to show up really badly. So thin your paint with water, or spirit, depending on what it is made of and spend ages stirring the thinner in until it is like single cream. Ignore what it says on the can about only adding 5 per cent water – they just want you to buy more paint. Use enough water to get it to a running cream consistency. You will need to use an extra coat but it dries beautifully, like velvet. An oil-based paint on woodwork will look like you sprayed it on.

rollers make a rubbish finish

However, they are really useful for just getting the paint onto the wall. Always brush over wet rolled paint lightly with a wide brush in every direction. You can't do much about the orange-peel ffect on your thighs but you don't have to have it on your walls!

running cream dries like velvet

first coats take longer

First coats take about twice as long as subsequent coats. It also takes more energy to get the first coat on – you can look forward to coats two and three gliding on much more easily.

prime

A good, quick-drying all-purpose primer will help to kill any stains and will also help the top coats of paint to dry properly. This is especially important for woodwork.

ceilings look better brushed

But if they are quite high you might get away with a roller finish of thinned paint. Try rolling the first coat and brushing the second. Brush towards the windows and you won't see so many of your track marks when the sun is shining.

trade paint dries quicker

And covers better for a cheaper price. This quick-drying property is the best tip you will ever get about paint. It's so quick-drying, in fact, that you can finish the first coat and get on with the second straight away.

which paint should you use?

The array of different paints can be confusing, but a chat with the owner of the paint shop will quickly guide you to the correct product. I used to have several different types of primer and undercoat in my store cupboard, but have come to realize that one good one will do all of the specialist jobs. It's white pigmented shellac, actually, but there are lots of good ones. It is difficult to put a water-based paint on top of an oil-based paint without major rubbing down, though, so try to keep your layers of paint in the same chemical family. Remember that thin is good. The more liquid a paint or varnish is, the smoother it will dry. Check out shellac. It's magic and has been around for years as the main ingredient of French polish. Try to get it as "three pound ready-mixed" (I won't bore you with an explanation).

"check out shellac, it's magic"

Emulsion	water-based	walls/ceilings
Eggshell	spirit-/water-based	woodwork/radiators/doors
Gloss	spirit-/water-based	woodwork/doors/metalwork
Primer	spirit-based	base coat on wood/metal, kills stains too
Varnish	spirit-based best	top coat for protection/ your choice of shine
Shellac	methylated spirits	varnish and stain sealer floors/woodwork
Heat-resistant	cellulose-based	black paint for barbecue/ fireplace edgings
Steam-resistant	water-based	bathroom/kitchen paint limited range of colours
Plaster matt coat	water-based	specially designed for new plaster/quick white coverage

order of work

As a general rule you should aim to work from top to bottom:

- Ceilings should come first, and probably the cornice at the same time. It's fine to bring the ceiling colour down onto the walls a bit, but do try to avoid leaving a thick band of the paint around the top of the walls – this will save you from having to sandpaper any brush marks away.

- Skirting, doors and door frames should have their first coat of paint next, so that you can paint over the edges a bit without worrying about being over accurate.

- Walls are the best bit because you can really see where the room is heading as soon as you start to colour the walls. Try not to paint over the edges onto the woodwork too much, though, because it might be difficult to cover with what is usually going to be a paler colour.

- Skirting and doors (and any radiators) get their topcoat of paint last. You will find that you are better at making straight edges in a certain way, and it's worth working with your best side, so to speak. I can paint a perfect straight edge around the top of a wall against the ceiling but not around the bottom. So I use the topcoat of skirting paint as my straight edge on skirting, and not the topcoat of the wall paint. Work with whatever is best for you and use as much masking tape as you need to. In time you'll stop using masking tape at all.

- Floors should be left right until the end. Put a coat of thick paint onto the floor, starting at the furthest corner from the door and paint your way out. You wouldn't paint yourself into a corner, would you? Adding a dash of terebene dryers (chemical dryers – you only need half a teaspoon) to your oil-based floor paint will help it to dry in half the time it says on the can. About 12 hours is best before you can walk on it, in bare feet only for a couple of days. Water-based will dry thoroughly for bare feet over night.

"don't paint yourself into a corner"

brush, roller, or gadget?

There is a plethora of different brushes and applicators for paint out there, but take a look in any professional's kit and you probably won't find anything out of the ordinary.

● the more brushes cost, the better the finish

Don't bother with any of the super-duper paint-spraying gizmo machines. Leave well alone the funky-syringe-type-sucky-squirty-stick on the shopping channels – just one more thing to go wrong and have to take back to the shop as far as I can see. At the risk of sounding like an old duffer, go for what has been tried and tested and re-purchased for many years.

In general, the more brushes cost, the better the finish will be. This is importantly true of woodwork brushes. Opposite are a few tips for deciding what you need and how to buy brushes.

"leave well alone the funky gizmo"

◨ Household paint brushes (for woodwork and emulsion)

Do buy natural flexible bristles, the longest you can afford

Don't buy one with a hole in the middle, these get too drippy

Look out for sash brushes with a light point – excellent for painting straight edges and window frames

Remember a big brush can get heavy so stick to 10–12cm (4–5in)

◨ Rollers (for getting paint on the wall quickly)

Do use a new roller for each different colour

Don't buy expensive ones and try cleaning them, they are impossible to clean fully

Look out for special offers on a cheap roller and tray

Remember to avoid the orange-peel effect by brushing over with light strokes of a good emulsion brush

◨ Odd-shaped handles (for getting to the awkward places)

Do have a couple of long-handled small brushes for getting behind pipes and radiators

Don't buy flash ones – you have to scrummage when getting behind things and the bristles go out of shape quickly

Look out for a basic brush on a long bent handle – perfect for getting right down behind radiators

Remember to keep a rag handy for wiping dust off the brushe

how much paint?

There will always be some details of coverage written on a can
of paint. This figure is usually a generous estimation, and you
needn't be too worried about buying exactly what it says. If
you are going to thin your paint you will be amazed how far
it goes, but you will need an extra coat for a good finish.

● thin your paint to make it go further

It is impossible to advise fully on how much paint you will need,
but if you think in terms of a 5 litre or gallon can of emulsion
getting you all the way around an average bedroom in two
coats you will be close. A roller takes lots of paint just to load
it up ready for use, so remember this when buying your paint.
Of course, if the paint is a really special mix and cannot be
repeated, then it is always wise to buy a larger can.

With woodwork paint for the doors and windows, the small
cans are usually enough for an average-sized room (about
4 sq m (4½ sq yd); any more tends to start drying up in the
can and it all gets a bit lumpy and messy. Varnishes go about
the same distance as woodwork paint – a 2.5 litre (½ gallon)
can will do two coats at least on a 16 sq m (17½ sq yd) floor.

wallpaper know-how

Wallpaper is coming back into fashion -- allegedly. We must brace ourselves for the onslaught of flowers and chintzy swirls again. It's a bit like olives isn't it? You either love wallpaper or you hate it. From the DIY point of view wallpaper can be a nightmare. Matching the patterns exactly and damage to the surface are the key issues.

- On some papers even the tiniest blob of wallpaper paste on the front will leave a mark. Try a little bit of glue on the front of a sample of any paper you are thinking of buying, just to make sure you can wipe it clean as you go.

- Wallpaper seams will need to be rubbed over when wet or the wallpaper will start lifting. Try rubbing the paper with a damp cloth and check for any unwanted shiny marks when it dries.

- When you wet a sheet of wallpaper with the paste and leave it to soak, the paper acquires a degree of stretch. This is useful for matching the patterns but can be really tricky if the paper stretches too much. You will need to buy a roll or two extra just to find out the best amount of time to leave the paste soaking in.

- It is very important to keep your cutting knife sharp for a clean edge. Wallpaper cutters come with snap-off blades, and there is no room for economy with these. Use a new blade for about every 1 m (40 in) of cutting.

- When choosing a design remember that the bigger the pattern repeat, the more paper you will need in order to match the pattern at the seams. In a normal-height room of about 230 cm, floor to ceiling, one roll of plain paper (with no pattern repeat) will cover about four drops.

lining paper

This is marvellous stuff for giving you a nice smooth surface to paint on. You must still pay attention to filling and smoothing before you line, though, as lining paper doesn't really hide the lumps. The ones where you put the paste onto the wall are actually pretty good, although pricey – excellent if you get in a dreadful pickle trying to put wet paper up onto a ceiling, because you can apply it direct onto the ceiling.

• lining paper is marvellous for giving a nice smooth surface to paint on

masking and mastic magic

Oh oh oh, the best tip in the history of decorating. USE MASTIC!

Mastic is a kind of soft rubbery compound that you squeeze from a tube or gun and use as final edging filler. Sometimes called caulk, and odd things like "decorators' friend", it is a bit like that sealer for around the edges of baths and showers. However, you can paint mastic and you cannot paint silicone bath sealants.

If you go into a professional supplier you will see boxes and boxes of mastic for sale. A high-street DIY store will often have only a single row on the shelves. Don't shoot the messenger, it is a fact that the professionals use lots of mastic and the amateurs don't.

Apply mastic around all edges of a room; around the door frame, along the skirting and around the top. A thin bead is all that is needed. Wipe your wet finger along it as you go and it will smooth nicely into the joins. Then, if it is still a bit proud, wipe it gently with a damp cloth. You will soon get the hang of it – it's not rocket science, but it makes so much difference. Use mastic after all of your other preparations because it is not sandable and can pick up dust. It is brilliant after putting up lining paper if you have missed a bit or have a slightly tatty edge

• apply mastic around all the edges of a room

Masking tape is the other way around: loads of it is sold in general DIY stores but you will only find the odd box for sale in the trade suppliers. Masking tape is great if you are a bit nervous of your painting skills, but it takes forever to put up and it can "bleed", so the paint goes behind it anyway. I find it better to work slowly and carefully around a tricky bit of painting, unless it's a valuable wood finish I am trying to protect, or the carpet! If you do use masking tape, don't assume it is doing what you want it to, and do paint carefully all the same. Use the cheapest one you can find because it will be less sticky and might not pull off quite so much of the paintwork when you take it off. Special low tack tapes are available and they're really good but costly.

It only takes practice and you will soon stop buying so much masking tape. Then you can spend your savings on lovely mastic instead!

tiling know-how

A girl gets asked to do her first tiling job and is told she can choose the tiles herself, and is given a fistful of money to spend on them. So she goes off to the designer showroom and chooses a disgustingly expensive one that is hand-made and fired in kilns fuelled only with rare wood chippings.

She starts to glue them to the wall and they look exquisite. Then she gets to the last one of the first row and it needs cutting. She measures it, puts it under the tile cutter and it breaks right across the middle. Twelve tiles later they are still breaking so she throws her tools down and goes off to a big commercial tile centre. Secretly she buys a batch of tiles made by a very big name in the world of tiles and they cost half the price but they look about the same.

When she gets back to the workshop she hides all of the posh tiles and puts up the less expensive ones, which cut really easily and she actually enjoys working with them. When the job is finished everybody loves the tiling and they all live happily ever after. The moral of this story is: get a sample tile or two and test how they cut before you buy the whole lot. Hand-fired tiles can be the end of your good nature and temper.

tiling

Tiling is easy if you have prepared the wall to a nice, even finish but here are a few tips you might appreciate:

 Once you have put the glue onto the wall, offer the tile up to it diagonally and sort of screw it round into the straight position. This really helps them to stick more firmly.

 As far as possible, keep the cut edges to less visible areas, such as the corners of the room or the window frames. Use the one smooth edge on every tile for ends where there will not be a tile next to them.

 A pair of tile nippers is good for gently nibbling a shape out of a tile. Just work in tiny little bites and you can cut any shape you need.

 Use a spirit level regularly because the grouting will show up any un-level work quite badly.

grouting

Some tile adhesives are also the grouting, and these make life a doddle.

Apply the paste evenly into all of the spaces.

" hand-fired tiles can be the end

- Push it in by swiping a grouting squeegee over the spaces.
- Wipe repeatedly with a wet cloth and keep rinsing it until the grouting is smooth and just below the level of the tile surface.
- It is OK to leave a fine powdery covering of grouting on the front of the tiles as this will wipe off and polish up when dry (just buff up with a cloth).

Old grouting can be cleaned either by removing it with a blunt-edged knife and re-grouting, which is like having new tiles again, or, if you want to avoid having to take the old grouting out, there are some paint-like products especially made for revitalizing grubby grouting. You just paint every seam, leave it to dry and polish it off. The effect is not as good as re-grouting, but the paint does make a significant impact and is definitely worth a try.

replacing tiles

If you have a broken tile and have a replacement available, then there is a way of taking out one tile only. It's a ten-minute job but can be dangerous so do wear eye protection and rubber gloves:

- Put a layer of masking tape over the whole of the tile to be replaced and hit it a few times with a hammer.

of your good nature and temper"

- The tile will crack all over, and you will be able to take it out piece by piece and stick a new one in the space.

- It's worth scraping off all of the old dry glue completely to give yourself a nice flat surface on which to put the new tile. If you use a combined glue and grout, you will be able to grout the new one in at the same time.

• existing tiles make for a good flat surface on which to apply the new ones

If, on the other hand, the whole wall of tiles really needs replacing, you could find yourself removing all of the old ones and then spending ages scraping off dried-up adhesive before you can re-tile. It might have to be done that way, but you can tile over the top of old tiles, and indeed this is recommended if the wall underneath is unsound.

Existing tiles make for a good flat surface on which to apply the new ones. However, your new tiled wall will be twice as thick as before so you will need a decorative edge piece to hide the evidence. If it's a whole wall, with tiles all over and right up to the edge, then just go for it and save yourself a day or two of horrible scraping and loading the car up with old tiles for the dump.

flooring

types of flooring

The state of the floors in any home has a huge impact on the overall image. Of course they should really be attended to last of all, after all of the mucky wet work such as painting and plastering has been done, but if you are sitting gloomily in your home wondering how on earth you will ever be able to make it look any better, then try looking down, pull up a corner of the floor covering, and look underneath.

floorboards

Yippee! This is easy. Carpets are often the reason for a bad smell in the house, and if they are not even good to look at then they have to go. Rip up the carpet in one room at a time and slice it into manageable sections with a craft knife. Get the whole lot down to the dump immediately. When you get back, sweep up and just wash the floorboards at this stage with a good old mop and bucket. Overdose the water with that special soap for wood, which is in all the supermarkets – magic. It's only cosmetic, and you might even like to give them a quick coat of furniture oil or paint for good measure before you go to bed tonight. There's still loads of real work to do on the floors, but just getting the carpet out and cleaning makes a huge difference.

"floorboards? yippee!"

flat wooden hardboard

Oh, you lucky girl. This floor is probably flat enough for you
to put down a hardwood or laminate floor on top of it, in time.
Once the carpet is gone and you have swept up, I suggest you
larrup a coat of water-based eggshell paint down in a neutral
colour and go to bed, or out on the town for a few hours, while it
dries. Painted floors can withstand a lot of heavy activity and
only need mopping and the occasional re-coat. I still have my
emergency white-painted floorboards despite all the DIY activity
and a big dog. I eventually filled all the cracks with caulk and
they get re-coated with paint about twice a year. You can mop
with bleach and you don't need a vacuum cleaner!

concrete

Yuk spluk, the worst-case scenario and you are going to need
some cheap rugs if you are going to manage without a carpet
for a while. Concrete floors are cold and unwelcoming. Things
break when you drop them on concrete too, but you could
leave the underlay down and just get rid of the actual nasty
carpet. Alternatively, you could paint with garage floor paint
which is available in all colours, not just dark red and grey.

carpets

If you are sticking with carpets then cleaning them will at least make the most of what you have. Get it done professionally if you can afford to. If you are on a tight budget, the carpet cleaners that you can hire for a day or two are nearly as good as the professionals. There is something so satisfying about watching the reservoir fill up with filthy water. Hired rug cleaners are heavy and noisy, but they have a powerful suction so you will be able to get the carpet almost dry by running over it with the cleaner on suction only a few times after it has come up clean.

Spot cleaning of a mark or spill can sometimes leave a clean spot, obliging you to do the whole room. As a rule you should soak up a spill thoroughly with clean cloths; stand on them to get as much up as possible. Then clean the spot using a carpet spot cleaner, but remember to work from the outside of the spill towards the middle. If you work from the middle out you will just spread the stain out further. After spot cleaning make sure you rinse the area well with a clean, damp cloth. Carpet shampoo left in the fibres gets dirty really quickly.

how much flooring to buy?

Take a good, accurate floor plan of the area you want to cover with you to the shop and let the trained sales staff help you. The flooring world is so competitive these days that you will probably get the fitting thrown in free for basic carpets and rubber-type floorings. Laminates are a different kettle of fish though, and fitting costs by the square metre.

Working out how much you need can be a peaceful evening job, allowing you to visualize the dramatic change that a new flooring is going to bring.

First, draw a diagram of the floor on a piece of paper; use your eye to get it as much to scale as possible. Then measure along the edges of the room and write the dimensions on the drawing.

● measure everything at least twice

Broadly speaking, you only have to multiply the width of the room by the length and the result is the square metreage of the room. So, 4 m wide by 5 m long is 20 sq m (22 sq yd). For carpets and rubber floorings that's it. Any cut-outs for fireplaces and fitted cupboards will be leftovers. Most carpets come in wide enough rolls for you not to have to seam.

estimating laminates and tiles

Because of the expense, you'll need to be accurate when working out how much laminate or tiling to buy. If your room is an L-shape, divide your floor plan diagram into separate portions – both sections of the L, for example. Work out the square metreage for each section and then add them together.

However, you might want a full run of the laminate flooring right through the two or more sections. If this is the case, measure out the biggest square area you can get for the first calculation and then add the odd edges and corners to it.

Laminates generally butt up to each other nicely only if you use the manufactured edges against each other, and on top of that they only work in one direction. So you need to buy enough laminate to avoid having to use your cut edges anywhere except up against the edge of the room. I can't stress this enough. Having chosen the laminate you would like, read the instructions carefully and find out exactly what you are dealing with. If in doubt, buy some extra packs when you order. The shade may change by the time you go back for more.

laminates

Laminate flooring is only as good as the money you spend on it. Oh yes, the lifetime guarantee on every pack: read the small print and you will find that they take no responsibility for the way in which it is fitted and used. Do you think I'll ever get my money back for the kitchen floor that I dropped a hammer on?

Mostly, laminate floorings are a chipboard backing with a tiny film of wood veneer on top, and then a topping of hardwearing plastic (laminate of course). Chipboard absorbs moisture like a sponge and swells up when wet. This has a major bearing on where you can use laminate, and it isn't really suitable for kitchens and bathrooms.

If you are adept at measuring and cutting then you'll have no problem putting a laminate floor down. Go for glueless: they just click together and you cover all of the easy bits in record time. The edges take longer, but you don't need more than a day for a living room.

Oh, remember that wood expands and contacts with temperature changes, so do bring the packs into the room for a couple of days before fitting them. Then the wood can settle down to the temperature of the room before it is fitted.

hardwood

Hardwood floors are the elite of wooden flooring. The thicker the better, the older the better; when wood has been well seasoned it will no longer need to breathe and change shape. Fitting a hardwood floor is really a professional job – when you're spending that much on the materials, let someone else take responsibility. But if you want to do it yourself, here are a few top tips:

- Use a hired pin gun with the thinnest pins (nails) you can. Fill the pin holes with wood filler and gently rub the fills down.
- Know where your pipes and cables are lurking under the floors, and don't pin through them.
- Pin into the joists. A look at the existing floorboards' nails will help you to locate them.
- Work in the opposite direction to the joists; the support of the joists is really important.
- Work right up to the edge of the room and put the skirting on after (this is a dream way of hiding any tatty edges).
- Don't go too tight to the edges – use a 1.5 cm strip of cork at the extreme edges to allow for some movement.

● fitting a hardwood floor is really a professional job

restoring old floorboards

sanding

Good old floorboards! Thank goodness somebody made a
fashion out of having them visible. You can hire a big sander
to bring them back to life, and there's nothing better than taking
off the top layer of dirty wood to reveal the new surface below.
They are great if you have a huge room to treat and if you have
spent three days taking out any nails and pins that will otherwise
rip the expensive sanding sheets to bits in two seconds flat. But
if not you will spend half an hour with the sander upside down,
un-jamming it, before putting another sheet in and having it
happen all over again. This is all at the same time as dealing
with angry neighbours who cannot bear the noise. The best thing
to use is a hired edging sander – these are much more gutsy
than domestic sanders, and the band variety are good if you
use them along the grain of the wood. Or use a circular sander.

safety

- This is messy, noisy work and you must mask your face and
  eyes well, even if you look like something out of *Star Wars*.
- Use three grades of paper: coarse, medium, and a lovely
  fine one for the last zizz over.

don't forget to work your way out

- When you have the finish you want, then all that remains is a satisfying coat, or five, of varnish (yep, the more the better).Just remember to work your way out of the room!

- Try shellac: old-fashioned, traditional, and dries in an hour.

painting

If you are going to paint the floor you won't need to worry quite so much about the final sanding, so long as the floor feels smooth to the touch.

- With painted floors, the more paint you build up on them the better they look, and you will gradually even out the finish as you apply more coats in months to come.

- Try filling the gaps between the boards with lovely mastic (*see* p47) before painting. This is a great way of keeping draughts at bay and of stopping the dirt coming up from down below.

- What type of paint? You will need to prime first, with any recommended undercoat or wood primer, and then oil-based eggshell is best but takes longest to dry; water-based eggshell is not bad and will dry overnight.

soundproofing

There are laws against Justin Timberlake at top volume and nothing is going to protect you from the Noise Abatement Society if you are one of those who play loud music at three in the morning. But there are quite a few ways of damping down the sound of heeled shoes and general household noises.

floors

If you live in a terrace or semi you might be aware of exactly what time your neighbours go to bed, and maybe you can hear their phone ringing or the light switches clicking on and off. My big concern was that they could hear me; careful investigation and playing around with various old blankets helped me to work out that most of the sound travels under the floorboards. The sound of switches comes from next door's conduit (the pipes that the cable runs through), and all of it seems to run down and come through the floor. Carpet is the best sound-proofer, of course, but it's not always a practical solution. A thick underlay increases soundproofing. Next best is cork flooring (mmm, lovely). Fabrics and soft furnishings also help to absorb sound.

Skirting boards sometimes have a big gap in the plaster behind them, and sound travels freely between you and next door through this thin area. If you find that your place was plastered only down to about 10 cm (4 in) above ground level, fill this with plaster or expandable filler, then replace the skirting, and you will really help to cut out some of the noise interference. In a perfect world you could get your neighbours to do the same.

**● carpet is the best soundproofer
but it's not always practical**

walls

If walls are thin then you are faced with losing a little bit of room space by lining them with sheets of plasterboard. The thicker the walls, the less sound you will hear. Plasterboard sheets are easy to cut with a normal hand-saw. Just remember "measure it twice, cut it once". For brick walls you will need to put up some wooden batons by screwing them firmly to the walls, and then attach the plasterboard to these. Keep the gaps between wall and plaster- board as narrow as possible. For bad noise cases fill the gap with expandable filler or fireproof wadding. For wooden-framed walls you can attach into the existing wood frame and get right up against the existing wall. Polystyrene is a great soundproofer and good as wadding, but pay the extra for fireproof, please.

fixtures and fittings

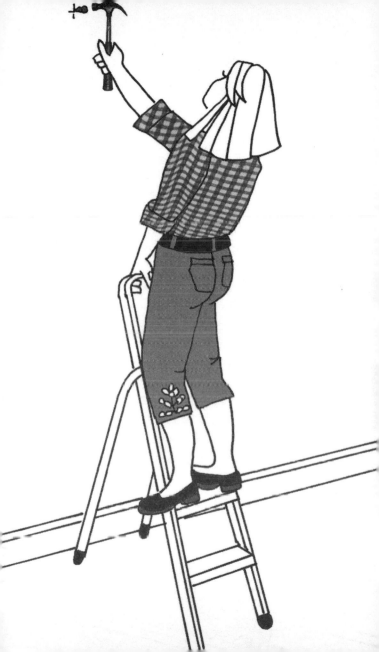

shelves and cabinets

Permanent fixtures such as shelves and cabinets seem to make a home look much more "finished" than a pile of trendy storage boxes in the corner. The only problem with them is that they are static, and if you are one of those girls who moves the furniture around once a week then you'd do well to keep to a minimum of these. Incidentally, did you know that moving the furniture around is a sign of being unsettled?

■ A mirrored cabinet can work wonders, serving as storage and bouncing extra light around the room, so consider using one, no matter how slim, in any place where you are tempted to put up a mirror.

■ Hide storage behind a picture: a slim cupboard can be hidden behind a picture, so long as you're not going to hit your head on it every time you walk past, as it will obviously stand about three inches proud from the wall. These are useful spaces for storing valuables, or items that you're not going to need on a regular basis.

Get to grips with the different types of fixings (see pp81–83) so that you only have to put something up once. And don't forget redundant ceiling space – great for hanging rails and baskets.

measuring

Repeat after me: "MEASURE IT TWICE AND CUT IT ONCE!"
Say this over and over as you are cleaning your teeth. In truth,
when you are measuring for something important then you will
automatically measure more than once. After you've made the
first expensive mistake that is.

● always carry your household measurements around with you

Treat yourself to a good long tape measure, one of those that
retracts back into itself at the touch of a button and has a hook
for your belt on it. If you are one of those people who lose
things then get a fluorescent-coloured one. You can see it
easily in the bottom of your handbag or toolbox. The cheap
ones seem to lose their numbers rather too quickly. Be aware
of a baggy end stopper on the tape – this is critical only when
you are precision measuring, but that end stopper can add a
couple of mm (fraction of an inch) if it is very loose.

" buy a good long tape measure "

measuring tips

- The most important is to measure it twice and cut it once.

- You will lose a small amount into sawdust when cutting wood, so always cut just outside any line you draw so that you lose only on the waste side and not on the shelf you are cutting.

- Also, measure and mark every time, rather than being tempted to use a cut bit as a template. You could gradually lose size by not re-measuring every piece.

- Templates are useful for odd shapes, and pressing a piece of newspaper into an irregular shape is a good way of starting a template. Then cut it out of slightly thicker card with less bend to it, such as a cereal box, and test it before marking and cutting the real thing.

One day you will see something in a shop that you would like to buy, but are not sure if it will fit into the corner you have in mind. It's a good idea to carry your household measurements around with you in a notebook or organizer. My trick is to store them in the mobile phone memory.

how to put up curtain rods

Every curtain rod is designed to hold a certain weight, so check the packaging. Some of today's thin poles are really strong and can bear a considerable amount of weight. Even thin wooden ones might be strengthened, allowing you to use less bulky rods. Your fixings will not only have to hold the weight of the curtains, but will also suffer stress every time you close or open the curtains, so they need to be strong.

- Check out the fixings section for ideas (*see* pp81-83), and if you hit a metal joist above the window when drilling, don't panic. Just change to a special drill bit for metal, and perhaps use a hammer type drill, or get the bloke from next door to help. You absolutely must get the fixings all the way in, so don't be tempted to stop short just because the going gets a bit tough.

- Use a spirit level to check that everything is straight. Some ceilings are not level, and obviously it is key that your rods are properly straight so that your curtains don't end up all on one side. If you don't have a spirit level then a mineral water bottle half filled with water is a reasonable botch. Best of all though is a clear tube of about 2 m (2 yd) in length, half filled with water. Hold up the two ends and the water will level itself.

blinds

A fitted blind will have a real impact on the finish of your windows.

how to shorten a blind

You can shorten a venetian blind to fit by spreading it out
on the floor, very carefully removing the cord stoppers along
the bottom of it, and removing any spare slats. Cut away the
excesses of the thread supports and tuck the new ends back
in, just the way it was made. Whatever you do don't pick
it up until you have re-secured the pull cords or it will all go
horribly wrong. Think as you go. This is best done without
interruptions and you don't want to take too much off. Just
carefully copy the way the blind was put together in the first
place but remove a few slats   fantastic tailor-made look in
about half an hour.

where to hang a blind

If your windows have a deep recess then you get to choose
whether to hang your blinds inside the recess or outside. Inside,
right up against the window glass, is best for heat insulation;
outside gives a smooth line against the walls. Ready-made blinds
will sit best outside because the measurement between the
brackets does not then need to be an exact fit within the recess.

how to drill a tile

There will come a time when you need to drill a neat hole in a tile so that you can put up a fixture. If you can arrange to go between the tiles where the grouting is, then you have the best cop-out possible. But sometimes you just have to get it right through an existing tile.

● put a cross of masking tape over the spot where you need the hole to be

■ You will need a masonry drill bit in your drill, and you should work with the drill on fairly slow. Keep to the smallest drill bit possible, as ever. Because there is a real danger of cracking the whole tile, put a cross of thick masking tape over the spot where you need the hole to be, and drill through tape, tile, and wall together.

● mark the length of the wall plug on the drill bit to check the depth

■ You must use a wall plug before putting the screw in, and it follows that the hole must be deep enough but not too deep. Try marking the length of the wall plug onto the drill bit so that you can see how deep you need to go.

how to put up
a cabinet

Any cabinet is only going to be as strong as its fixings, just as a chain is only as strong as its weakest link. The worst-case scenario is the wall cupboard in the kitchen, full of heavy tins of soup and condiments, so let's look at that and then you can modify downwards for that little key cupboard you want to put up by the front door.

The secret of fixings is the amount of grip they have in the wall – rock solid if possible. The other factor is the strength of the backing board you are fixing through. Let's assume that the manufacturer took that into consideration. Have you noticed that fixtures are often supplied without the fixings? This is so that the supplier doesn't get held responsible for how you put it up. Go for the strongest fixings.

▣ Wall bolts are like wall plugs but much tougher, and made of steel. As you screw the big screw into them they open up, a bit like an umbrella, and eventually are forced open as much as the hole in the wall will allow. They grip. Drill holes for the wall bolts as deep as the entire length of the bolt (measure the bolt against your drill bit), as small as you can so they are not loose, and then hammer the new, virgin wall bolt home firmly. The deeper the wall bolt, the more secure your fixing will be. One that has already been opened is bad news so bin it. Screw the fixing up through the back of the cabinet and right down snug into the wall bolt. This takes major effort and grunting noises. You are working against the pressure of the opening bolt inside the wall, so this is a good sign. The harder it is the better the fixing, within reason. Most important is that the screw goes all the way home.

● the deeper the wall bolt, the more secure your fixing will be

● A spirit level will come in handy, and sometimes putting a round pencil sideways on a shelf will help to see if you are level. If it rolls then you know which way to adjust the cabinet.

● A big cupboard will need two people. This is one of those times when you might have to encounter someone who thinks they have better ideas than yours. Getting everything ready before asking and laying out the wall bolts, drill, etc ready for action can sometimes help ease the stress of working in DIY pairs. Mark up the positions for the holes yourself and do as much as you can before getting the crew in.

how to hang a picture

This is so easy compared to some of the things you will find yourself doing, and it is one of those steps towards a finished home that you will notice every time you walk into a room.

- Decide exactly where you want the picture to hang and mark the wall lightly with a faint pencil line at the top.

- Work out the width of the picture – anything wider than about 80 cm (31½ in) should have two or more hooks. Use a spirit level to help when you mark the position of the hooks.

- If the height of the top of the picture is critical then this measuring trick might help you: hold your tape measure under the wire on the picture and measure the distance to the top with the wire tense, as if it were already hanging. This tells you the distance down from the mark you have made on the wall to the bottom of the hook. Repeat this for each hook.

- Picture hooks should go into the wall with the nails at a slight downward angle, not horizontal, to give them extra strength.

- For seriously heavy items, screws into good firm wall plugs will be miles stronger. Always double up by bashing a couple of big nails into the wall a few inches below the real fixings – the nails may help to stop or slow the picture if it falls.

which fixings for what job?

plugs, bolts, hooks, and nails

Wall plugs: little plastic plugs that give you a grip against the threads of the screws and against the inside of the hole you have drilled.

Expandable wall plugs: the next step up – use them all the time if you can. They are just like wall plugs but they scrunch up and really fill the hole as you insert the screw.

Cavity plugs: good for ceilings and cavity walls, these open up like an umbrella once they are inside the hole and give a good grip in holes where a wall plug would just fall down inside.

Wall bolts: seriously tough wall fixings, used on building sites around the world, these also open up as you insert the screw or bolt; remember, the deeper the plug the more secure the fixing will be.

Ribbed nails: nails with little ribs on them that are great for gripping into wood but not very pretty; difficult to pull out if you change your mind about having used one, but great in the shed or the garage.

Nail-substitute glue: good for fixing long strips of wood such as skirting board; double up with nails while you wait for it to dry.

Hooks: good-quality hooks with a sharp thread will fix direct into wood without the need for plugs or special extras. If they screw in easily then the fixing will not be strong – tough is good.

screws

Cross heads: the most common and the easiest to screw in, they have a little cross indent for your screwdriver. For joining two bits of wood, look for ones where the thread goes all the way to the head, otherwise they are fine with the thread ending 1 cm (½ in) or so before the head.

Flat head screws: the bit you see when the screw is in place is flat, rather than rounded.

Round heads: the bit you see is a little dome that sticks up slightly.

Countersunk screws: the heads go right into the wood, but you need to drill a countersink for it with a special drill bit; they create a nice neat finish.

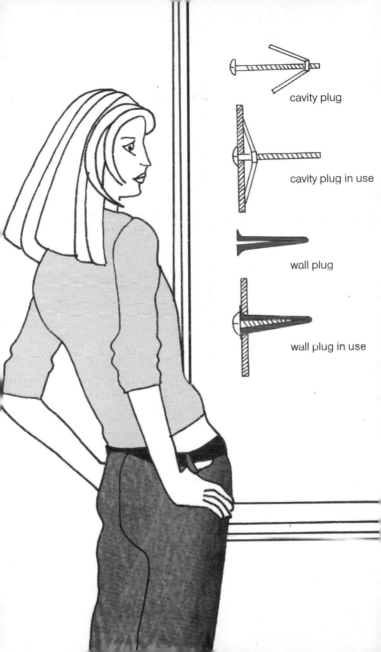

cavity plug

cavity plug in use

wall plug

wall plug in use

shelving and storage

shelve the lot

This isn't frivolous spending; you have to have shelving and storage, so you might as well go for something you really like first time round.

If you look in the shops and catalogues you will quickly come to realize that this is a big corner of the DIY market. From garage shelving to hat boxes, every storage need is catered for. Most of it comes flat-packed and all you need is a screwdriver. So let's measure the space and get on with it.

One of the first considerations must be what you want the shelving and storage for. Decorative or functional? Heavy-duty kitchen paraphernalia or underwear and socks filing? Wood, glass, or something fancy like polished steel?

If you are filling an existing space in a cupboard with some extra drawers or shelves then you can probably find exactly what you need in the shops. Ready-to-assemble kits come in all manner of shapes and sizes. However, if you are having to buy something that will be visible, say shoe storage for example, then look a little closer at the choices. There are some clever ideas out there – for example, shoe storage needn't be just a wire shoe rack, it could also double up as a telephone table.

flat-packed kits

These are pretty self-explanatory, but are unlikely to come with the wall fixings in the pack. Assembly is boring work, so make sure you do it properly the first time:

- Get the joins as close as you can.

- Re-tighten any joints after a couple of weeks and again after about six weeks, as they tend to move and loosen quite a bit when they are still new.

- In the case of flat-packed wardrobes and tall workstations, there's a limit to how tall you can build something on the floor. The ceiling might get in the way as you try to lift it into position, and you could end up taking it apart and re-building it in a standing position. Sometimes the manufacturer will provide information on minimum ceiling heights, but they're not all so helpful. Just a point to bear in mind ...

- Decide where to position the shelves of any adjustable kit by measuring up against things you need to store, such as your tallest book or tallest bottle of cooking oil. Cereal boxes are often the tallest things in the kitchen cupboard, so you could use them as a guideline.

● measure the items you need to store

how to
make your own

Making your own storage out of wood and batons means
you can fit a shelf into the most awkward of spaces.

cutting a straight edge with a jig-saw

Using a faint pencil line, measure and mark the wood exactly.
A jig-saw is a hand-held tool, so is only as straight in cutting as
your hand is steady – not very in most cases. Measure up the
width of your jig-saw between the edge and the blade, clamp
a bit of wood onto the piece you are cutting, then run the saw
along it, and take the guesswork out of keeping it straight.

right-angled joins

When joining two bits of wood at right angles there are natty little
plastic blocks that make it a doddle. The holes in them guide the
screws into position and make a reasonably firm right-angled
join. But they're not strong enough to support heavy items and
aren't very pretty, so only use them if they're hidden from sight.

for heavy books, etc

Use a wooden baton fixed securely to the wall all the way along
the length and width of the shelf. Get those batons screwed in
nice and deep with good-quality wall plugs (see p81).

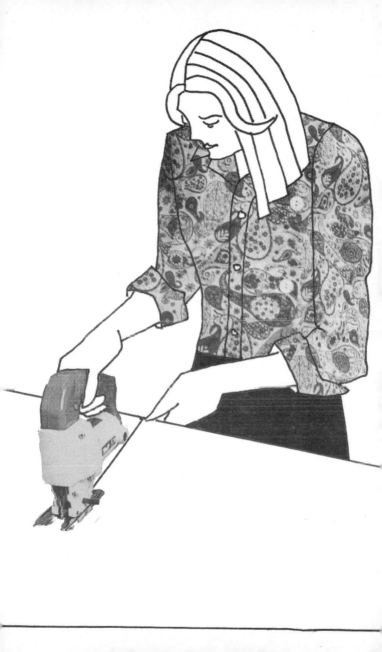

buying wood

Wood is expensive, and, as with most things in life, you get what you pay for. The grain of a wood tells some of its story; for example, those with the grain far apart have been given plenty of water to drink and really forced to grow. One grain mark represents just one winter when the tree has to toughen up against the cold. Fast-grown (soft) wood is generally of poorer quality. Slow-grown and tight-grained woods are harder and less likely to bow as they get older than soft woods.

Wood is seasoned by being left to dry naturally and slowly in a good airflow. Ask any wood carver and they will tell you that wood should be seasoned for at least two years – five years is best – before they would consider working with it. Cheap wood may well bend and split once it is in your home, because it has not been allowed to dry out and mature at a steady pace.

Compound woods, such as MDF and superwood, are made of wood and paper particles pressed together with glue. They are not available in the USA because there is a possible health issue as you must not breathe the dust. The more expensive varieties are harder, made of more particles and less glue. The green variety is suitable for bathrooms and is waterproof (ish).

treating wood

If you leave wood untreated you may see it start to split and bend.
It needs a drink of wood preservative every couple of years:

shellac

This is thinned with methylated spirits and it dries really fast.
You can make your own from shellac crystals dissolved
overnight in methylated spirits. It stinks to high heaven, so
open a few windows, and keep it well away from fire. Shellac
is hard-wearing but no good for anything on which you will
put a hot dish or wet glass, as this will leave a white mark.

waterproof finish

Use a polyurethane product; they are available in lots of different
wood shades, and you can build up a depth of colour with several
layers and then finish off or re-touch with a clear one. Exterior-
quality wood treatments are good for using indoors as well.

pure unglossy finish

This can be achieved by wiping over bare wood with a wood
oil, sometimes called Danish oil, teak oil, or tongue oil. It's
easy to apply, dries in 24 hours, and smells great. This is perfect
for garden furniture as well as chopping boards and skirting.

ceiling fixtures

If you are fixing into the ceiling you need to screw the fixing into a wooden joist. There are gadgets that help you to find cables and joists just by running them over the wall until a light comes on, but I have my doubts about them. A simple old hand drill with a tiny wood drill bit, like the one your Dad used to use, is best.

First you have to do that knocking thing which we've all seen done; knock on the wall or ceiling and listen to the sound. Near to a joist the sound changes from hollow to solid. This is a starter for the rest. Drill a tiny hole into the ceiling or wall and look for shavings of wood coming out of the drill bit. First you get plaster dust and then you should see wood shavings. If you don't, then move over a bit and try again. Yes, you have to fill the holes but they're so small that it's easy to just dab a fingerful of filler over them.

When you find wood, move around with the drill a little so that you can be sure to drill the real hole for the fixing right into the centre of the joist. Ceiling joists are so strong that you will be able to hang your whole body weight on a hook which is tightly secured into one. Actually, that is a test worth running before you hang your wine collection from the new fixture.

When drilling into a wood joist you should only need the toughness of a good hook – plugs and things are not necessary unless you drill the hole too big. As a rule of thumb, use a smaller drill bit and try screwing the hook in. If it really won't go in then make the hole a bit bigger and try again. Tight as can be. If you are not grunting with the energy of screwing the hook into the joist then it might not be tight enough.

• every fixing should be a bit stronger than the weight it is going to carry

Every fixing should be a bit stronger than the weight it is going to carry. For shelves, remember what you are going to put on them; for cabinets, what you might be putting in them. Water is very heavy, so allow for your big vases and oh, the fish tank …

"the most unlikely corners can

secret storage

Speaking from the point of view of an incurable minimalist, you understand, if you can create storage somewhere, then do so. The most unlikely corners can provide a tiny bit of storage space:

- Just between the sink and the meter cupboard in my kitchen there is a gap of about 15 cm (6 in). This wasted space now houses jars of mustard and oils. Result.

- When re-building the fireplace backing I set it nice and high so that I could watch the fire ticking over from the bed and loft a gap below it for the log storage.

- Never buy a divan bed unless it has at least four drawers in it.

- If your kitchen cupboards are those that leave a big gap between the top and the ceiling, you could raise them right up to the top of the wall and suspend an extra shelf below.

- Fancy rope through a polished plank of wood or glass hung from the underneath of the cupboard works well, although the knot inside the cupboard needs to be as flat as possible.

provide a tiny bit of storage space"

"it's all under the floorboards"

- Making sure that the washing machine is securely fixed in its place and not likely to go chugging around the house when it spins can sometimes free a little space to store the tea trays, or hang a towel in.

- The table on which your TV sits could easily be a trunk in which to keep items that you don't often use.

- Hinge the bath side panel from the bottom and use magnetic clips at the top, and you have instant access to the space beneath the bath. Not pretty enough for storing lotions and potions, but ideal for cleaning fluids and even your tool kit.

- The big secret of a minimalist home: it's all going on under the floorboards. There's a gap over 30 cm (12 in) deep and a good 1 m (39½ in) width between the joists of the upstairs floors. So some basic boxes can be suspended down to the joists, made using water-proofed plywood and a pin gun. Then the section of floorboard over them is hinged on one side and has a little finger-hole pull-up opposite the hinge. There are some hinged handles (often used on boats) where the pull-up lies flat inside the brassware. Take care that the floorboards rest on a joist, so that you don't go hurtling through the ceiling when you step on them.

odd shapes and corners

levelling

Most homes don't actually have perfectly level ceilings. So, when levelling another horizontal line you need to consider if you want to have it in line with the ceiling or perfectly level. Sometimes a compromise between the two is good; it might prevent either the ceiling or the new fixing from looking totally out of kilter.

The main tool you need for levelling is a basic, good-quality spirit level. About 1 m in length should serve you well for most jobs, and maybe a tiny one just for checking the top of pictures, mirrors, etc. A long level will have a horizontal bubble in it and a handy sideways or vertical one. Just line the bubble in the fluid up between the two middle lines and you have the level perfectly positioned.

> ● **the main tool you need for levelling is a basic, good-quality spirit level**

However, if you do find yourself without a spirit level you could try using a square plastic bottle half filled with water. For this you will need to lay the half-filled bottle down on a surface you already know to be level and mark where the edges of the water come to. Then you can use this as a guide at any height.

Alternatively, and this is a great trick for levelling up on both sides of a wall, take a long length of clear tubing and almost fill it with water. A lump of eraser is handy to stopper the ends. No matter how you hold the tube the ends of the water will always be level with each other. You can use this trick for levelling longer lengths such as one end of a wall to the other, and you can even tape the ends of the tube up onto the wall while you work. For non-critical levelling, a simple round pencil or candle will help. If it rolls the surface isn't level.

fitting

Getting fixtures and fittings into quirky corners can involve you in quite a bit of fiddly work, but it's worth it to make use of a dead area.

Sometimes your drill won't fit into the space where you need to make a hole, and the only way around this is to go in at an angle. If you do this, make sure you go in as deep as possible and use long plugs and screws. Also, try to drill in the opposite direction from the pull of the fixture. So, for a shelf, drill the holes at an angle from top to bottom, like a plane coming in to land, which will counter some of the downward pull of the

shelf. Keep the angles as slight as possible so that you don't
end up with half an inch of the screw visible.

● drill in the opposite direction
from the pull of the fixture

If it is a light-fitting you are working with, make sure there will
be enough space around the lamps. They give off heat and
will be hazardous if there is not enough air circulation.

cutting

Cutting a shelf to fit an odd shape is not impossible. Make sure
you give a bit of thought to how you will fix it first and then make
an accurate template of the shelf, first from paper, which is nice
and flexible so you can push it into the corners, and then from
something non-flexible. Make sure it fits and that you can get
it into position when it is finally cut from something thicker.

There are hundreds of corner cupboards and bathroom cabinets
available. You won't need to cut much for yourself unless you get
into the realms of shelving around the hot water tank or under the
bathroom sink. None of this is impossible, though. Remember to
make them easy to remove for work on plumbing and electrics.

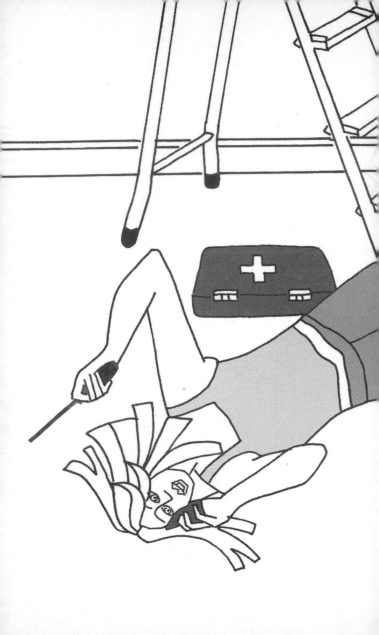

security and safety

things to think about

Your security and safety, as well as that of those around you, must surely be the most important consideration of all. If you live on your own it's even more crucial because there will not always be someone on hand to help you deal with an emergency.

In terms of safety, prevention is better than cure, but let's face it, there will be times when you have an accident or do something stupid. Won't there? Use your head and give some thought to what could go wrong. Make sure you have a well-stocked first-aid kit, and know how to use it. Promise me that you will stand only on safe, secure ladders and take no chances. If it's too scary then don't do it. And get a mobile phone to keep in your pocket as you work. If you fall it might not be possible to get to the door or the landline phone to summon help.

● always stand on safe, secure ladders

If you are about to tackle something that makes you feel nervous for your safety, the safe option is to get help or at least company. The extra stress involved in working alone at a high level, for example, could be the reason you fall.

ladders

Did you know that most muscle injuries for painters and
decorators are the result of sneezing while reaching out
from the top of a ladder? My physiotherapist told me that.
Over-reaching is dangerous, so move your steps and work
in a comfortable position.

Step ladders have locks on them that stop them from doing
the splits with you on board. Make locking your ladders a
habit and tell others "lock your steps please" on the many
occasions you see them working on unlocked steps.

falling

Make a wish that it never happens to you, but if you do find
yourself falling from a ladder or decorating platform then
RELAX. Our bodies are much more flexible and less likely to
break if we land as floppily as possible. When landing from
a height, even from jumping, land on your flat feet if you can
and use your legs and knees as springs to absorb some of
the impact. Just the way you see gymnasts landing. Nothing
is as important as your life … let the can of paint fly rather than
reaching out for it.

security

Your security is a serious subject. Try not to do business at the door. There are some weirdos out there who think a friendly attitude is a come-on. So follow your instincts. My pals play a tune on the knocker like a code, otherwise I don't answer it.

fitting a spy hole

A spy hole in the front door is very easy to fit: drill the right-sized hole and then screw the two sections together through the door. For an external door, two door locks, a simple cylinder type and a five-bar mortice lock, are the norm for most homes. It's a real bother if you need two hands to open your door, one on each key, so a mortice lock is great because you only have to turn the key and then you can let go of it.

fitting a security light

A security light that comes on at dusk or when you walk in front of it is a real comfort factor, because it helps you to get the key into the door, and comes on when someone else approaches the door. These are called PIR lights (passive infra-red), and they are no more difficult to fit than an indoor light fitting. Take advice on the cables if they are going to be exposed to the elements, though.

Battery-operated push lights will be suitable if you have a porch or shelter in which to put one, but they don't stand up to the weather.

● a security light that comes on at dusk or when you walk in front of it is a real comfort factor

fitting window locks

Window locks will keep your insurance premiums down and give you extra security. You can set them for locked shut, and some have a setting so that you can sleep with the windows ajar but nobody can get in.

fire escapes

Keeping intruders out is one thing, but how will you get out if your bedroom is on fire? Think about it. You can get a rope ladder to keep under the bed, but make sure you know how you will get it into position quickly.

The more security features you have, the less you will pay for your insurance. If your home needs to be like a fortress, though, why are you there? Peace of mind is priceless.

glass know-how

frosted glass

Have you ever been driving along in your car and seen someone
in an upstairs bathroom quite clearly? That glass made with a
sort of bubbled surface is actually quite see-through. Frosted
glass provides more privacy, so long as it isn't wet. In truth, the
uglier it is the more privacy it will provide. Check out the leafy
mess design that is so common and you will see what I mean.

frosting spray

You can frost glass for yourself with a spray. It really is good stuff:
just apply it in several thin coats as evenly as you can. Test your
glass by putting a few bottles of shampoo on the windowsill and
leaving the lights on, then go outside. Sometimes you can actually
read the labels; it'll make you blush if you've lived there a while.

toughened glass

This is more difficult to break and shatters into little cubes like a
car window, so there is less danger of injury if it does break – good
for mirrors. The best glass security is still the sealed double-
glazing unit, the type with an airtight pocket between the two
panes. Not only does this keep the heat in, but it makes an
almighty noise if it is broken, so burglars tend to leave it alone.

first-aid kit

Have one handy and replace anything you use. If you are completely clueless about first aid, check out some of the basics on the web or join an evening course run by the local voluntary ambulance service. Your workplace might even offer to send you on one if you agree to become one of their first-aiders.

The important ingredients of a DIYer's first-aid kit are really geared towards cuts and sprains:

- Sterile pads for pressing onto a wound; apply a pad and firm pressure to any cut.
- Sterile gauze for applying to a cut that is too big for a plaster.
- Lots of plaster tape for wrapping a dressing onto a wound and keeping the pressure on.
- Little plasters, especially the finger-shaped ones.
- Sterilizing spray, ouch.
- Crêpe bandages or athletic stretch supports for sprains.
- Scissors.
- Rub-in liniment for massaging into a bad ache.
- A torch.
- A note of the number for the doctor and the hospital.

phone a friend

Your mobile phone will quickly become your best friend, if it isn't already. If it is small enough to keep in your pocket you will be able to call for help much more easily than if it is in your handbag in the other room.

When you are working alone, though, sudden ringing can make you jump. When you're doing high-level or tricky work, don't switch it off but rather change the setting to silent for that period of time. Then you can still see if anyone has called you and you will still be able to dial out immediately.

Put important numbers at the top of the memory. Rather than paging down for "Mum" when you need help urgently, it's easier to find AaMum, as it will be the first entry in the memory.

" your best friend is a mobile phone "

electrics and plumbing

the backbone of your home

OK, most of your DIY activities can be planned and are a matter of choice. You decide on Thursday to knock down an old cupboard at the weekend. And of course you reserve the right to reschedule if you get a better offer. But if you get home to find a flood on the kitchen floor, or that the lights aren't working, you have to take immediate action.

The electrics and the plumbing in your home are just about the backbone of comfortable living. If they are not functioning properly we are miserable and hassled. There is no way of supplying you with enough information to cover every eventuality, so my advice is to take out the plumbing and electrical insurance offered to you by your gas and electricity company. It's a bargain! And remember to watch and learn every time you have a professional working in your home.

In the meantime, here are some basics that might help you to understand what you are dealing with.

electrics

What is electricity? We take it completely for granted but few of us really know what it is. Electricity is the movement of charged electrons through a conductor. Got it? The conductor is anything that conducts electricity, like a run of copper wire or your body. Think in terms of a hosepipe with lots of connections on it. When you turn on the tap the water is pushed through, and finds its way into all of the extensions. It turns corners, can overfill and burst the hose, and it can leak out of any holes. It's much the same for electricity except that the flow of charged atoms is caused by switching something on (the load) at the appliance rather than at the tap end of a hose. Electricity flows when you give it somewhere to go to. You, for example, are a brilliant conductor.

- **all parts of an electrical installation can be live and can kill you**

Do you think that the earth wires in your home are dead and not dangerous? Do you think the word neutral means harmless? STOP RIGHT HERE. All parts of an electrical installation can be live and can kill you.

The basics of electricity are the words voltage, amps, and watts. On the next page are definitions of what these are.

- Voltage is like the pressure of the electricity delivered to your home by the supplier. Most of us in the UK have the same voltage, but it varies from country to country.

- Amps, or amperes if we're being posh, is the current of the electricity or (sort of) the speed of the flow. Different appliances need different amounts of electricity to make them work and they will only draw what they need. A bit like turning the tap down to fill a teacup, and up to fill a bucket.

- Watts, or wattage, is the amount of electricity an appliance will use and we pay for our electricity in accordance with how much we have used. 1,000 watts is called a kilowatt hour and we pay by the hour. So, ten 100 watt light bulbs will use up 1 kilowatt in an hour and a three-bar heater at 2 kilowatts will use up a kilowatt hour, or unit, in half an hour. Electrical appliances usually have a label on them telling you the consumption.

So why have we just spent time on that? It's about fuses, or lifesavers, and it will all become clear soon.

knowing what went bang!

know your fuse board

There are still some really old fuse boards in many homes that are not quite so idiot-proof as the modern ones. Have a look inside your fuse box. If you have a main on/off switch and a row of other switches or breakers then you are probably more up to date than I am. However, if you find a main switch and a row of rectangular plugs with coloured stickers on them but no switches, then you probably have an old type re-wireable fuse board. These don't have a trip capability – all that happens is that the fuse blows. Big nuisance. You can convert an old fuse board yourself without a panic – just look for conversion switches in the DIY stores. All you have to do is take out the old rectangular plug fuse and put one in its place. Follow the colour coding when you buy them, as this is the ampage of the fuses inside and it's important that your different circuits are running on the correct ampage. So replace a white sticker with a white trip switch, and so on.

smile – be happy when a fuse blows

It might just have saved your life. Conductors heat up if too much current is going through them. This can result in fire and will damage electrical equipment such as your computer. The fuse is effectively a weak link in the circuit that will melt through, or "blow", so as to break the circuit. Putting a thicker link in to complete the circuit is plain stupid. Don't do it. The fuse is your messenger that something is wrong. The current might have re-routed to earth (there it is ... live current travelling down the earth wire that you thought was harmless) and this tells you that there is a wiring problem somewhere.

working out what went bang

Suddenly, you are mid-flow with the hairdryer and it stops. It could be that the fuse in the plug has blown, telling you that something is wrong with the hairdryer. If it's not really obvious, and there was no odd noise or smoke, you could replace the plug fuse with a new one of the correct ampage and try again. If it happens a second time then condemn the hairdryer.

If all the upstairs plug sockets go down at the same time then the problem has got itself further back into your system. Unplug what you can and re-set the trip (or replace the fuse wire in an old wylex). Try again. Gradually go round the house plugging appliances back in. If it blows again then you have

found the problem appliance. Beyond this, for example if you have unplugged everything and the fuse still trips, then you must seek professional help.

what fuse should I use?

This is where all the explanations about wattage, amps, and voltage become relevant. You can calculate the amperage of the fuse you require as watts divided by volts.

A hairdryer is 1,600 watts and the voltage into the house is 230 volts. So, 1,600/230 = 6.95 amps. There is no 6.95 amp fuse so use the next one up; a 10 amp fuse. Go no higher than the next one up. The other way around is to calculate how much an appliance is using: amps x volts = watts. The fan heater has a 10 amp fuse in it and the voltage is 230 volts: 10 x 230 = 2,300 watts. It uses 2.3 units of billed electricity in one hour, ouch. You should not have more than 1,000 watts of light bulbs on any lighting circuit, or a maximum of ten 100 watt light bulbs.

The higher the wattage the hotter they get, and you must take great care when choosing how bright a bulb you use, especially if you are using lampshades purchased separately. Most shades tell you the maximum watts for the light bulb.

socket safety

overloading sockets

If you need to use extension adaptors for day-to-day appliances because you don't have enough plug sockets, you should get the ring extended. Too many plugs into one socket can cause an overload problem. Things get hot under overload conditions, fuses might blow or the house might catch fire. Keep extension cables for occasional use; always unravel the reel completely before using it, because they heat up and you might get smoke.

converting a single socket into a double

A single socket can easily be converted into a double socket. Buy a kit from your electrical wholesaler, because you can be sure of good quality; the ones in the DIY stores will cost about the same but might not be as long-lasting. The detailed instructions in the packaging of converter kits are quite straightforward to follow but make sure you understand everything before you start.

- Draw a clear diagram of how the old one was connected, just in case you end up putting it back on.
- Switch off the power completely, not just the trip switch.
- Test that the sockets aren't working by plugging a lamp or something into one before you start.

clearing blockages

Yuk! We all have to do it some time, though, and if you can avoid having to get covered in slime then so much the better.

A little sink plunger is a good weapon to start with; put the rubber dome over the blocked plughole and pump the handle up and down. You will be creating suction in the pipe, which will most often be enough to shift the blockage and get the flow going. Well, a bit of the flow. Enough to follow up with one of the superb chemical drain cleaners, which you should be able to get from most supermarkets.

● creating suction in the pipe will usually shift the blockage and get the flow going

Failing that, it is time to get familiar with your U-bend madam. Immediately under the plughole of your sink you will find a little bit of plumbing, which, as the name suggests, is a U-shaped bend. This holds some water all the time and is there to stop the stink from the drain system coming back up into your house. You can put a bowl underneath it and unscrew it completely. Brace yourself for the slime and muck. Now you wouldn't rinse it out over the sink you have just taken it from, would you?

draining your water system

To stop a major leak or to work on your plumbing you may need to empty out the water. Here's what to do, with no frills, just in case you are reading this with wet towels on the floor around you.

ordinary water

- Switch off the mains water into the house. This will be a low-level tap against one of the outside walls. Try looking for it under the sink, by the boiler, or in the downstairs loo.

- Open all of your taps, take plugs out and let the water flow away. It should stop flowing in about 10 mins, emptying the main tank and the hot water cylinder in your airing cupboard.

- Meanwhile, look for any wheel-shaped taps (gate valves), especially in the airing cupboard or by the boiler. If you find any, close them; these are handy cut-offs for parts of the system. As soon as the panic is over, find out what they close off, for future reference.

central heating water

Try to avoid draining the central heating system if possible, but if there is a potential flood then follow these emergency measures:

- First switch off the electricity to the boiler controls.

- If the leak is in the central heating system and a bucket won't do, you must first prop the ballcock up to stop the expansion tank filling. The expansion tank (if you have one and most of us do) is a small tank in the loft, usually set up on a shelf or stand and close to the main tank. Use a bit of string around the arm of the ballcock and attach it to the beams somehow so that the arm cannot lower.

- Look for a "dog leg" bit of pipe under one of the downstairs radiators or by the boiler. Quickly attach a bit of garden hose to it (it has ridges so you can shore the pipe on it and push it firmly home), get the other end of the hose outside and open the little square screw thing on the dog leg. The mucky black water will drain away out of the system, preferably down a drain if you can get that far with the hose.

- As the water slows down, go round the house – upstairs first – and gently open the bleed valves on the side of each radiator. You need to let air into the system in order for the water to gravitate down.

- When the water stops flowing completely, close off the bleed valves but leave the hose on, just in case there is some residue still coming through.

ballcock problems

Ballcock mechanisms aren't what they used to be (so I'm told) and they do wear out after a few years. If you have problems you might need to replace it, but try adjusting it first.

dripping overflow

If your outside overflow pipe is dripping, this means the tank is too full. The ball on a ballcock floats and should shut off the incoming water when it is full. If it doesn't, you need to get it so that it shuts off sooner by lowering it. Push the ball down a bit and turn the screw at the other end of the arm a couple of times, which will make it longer. It's trial and error, but the longer the screw against the shut-off valve, the sooner it will stop the incoming water. You don't need an empty cistern to do this.

getting a better flush

You can also increase the level of fill in the tank for a better flush on the loo by shortening the screw. Watch for the overflow level though (the little pipe sticking up above the water level).

Never over-tighten plastic joints. And, when buying a ballcock mechanism, make sure you remember what your existing one looks like and which side of the tank the water comes in.

"... aren't what they used to be"

basic plumbing jobs

how to fix a dripping tap

These are easy to remedy, especially if you have isolation valves.
An isolation valve is a straight joint in a pipe with a tiny flat-head
screw top in the middle of it. If the screwdriver indent is in line with
the pipe the water is on, and if it is at right angles to the pipe
the water is off. Isolation valves are probably the most magical
bit of plumbing kit ever. You can stop the flow to the individual
tap you are working on without having to drain down the system.
You can switch them all off when you go away. I can't recommend
these highly enough, and hope that you are lucky enough to have
them already. If not, treat yourself and have a plumber put them in.

- Stop the flow to the tap and you can take it apart quite easily.

- Start with the screw underneath the decorative hot or cold
  button and work down, unscrewing any bits of the outside
  of the tap you can until the innards are clearly visible.

- You'll find washers on the internal workings, which you can
  replace in the wink of an eye.

- I have always just taken out the whole innards of the tap,
  which unscrew in one piece, and gone down to the trade

suppliers with it. They'll know if it's just a washer issue or whether to send you home with a new inner mechanism for a good price.

 Bung it back in nice and tight and it's done.

 When putting plumbing back together you might need to wrap a bit of PTFE around the threads. PTFE is a fine white tape, which kind of wiggles itself into the joints as you join them. It stops tiny and annoying leaks by sealing the threads.

how to bleed a radiator

At the top of the radiator there is a square screw valve. This valve should be opened every few weeks using the special bleeding key. It's a simple bit of maintenance, but it will keep banging noises from air locks at bay, and your radiators nice and hot:

 Open the valve about one turn, holding a cloth just under it.

 Listen to any air coming out of the radiator – if you're doing it for the first time it might take a minute or two to all come out.

 When water starts to trickle out it means all the air has gone; just close up the valve and move on to the next one.

solving noisy plumbing

If it really sounds like a kettle boiling and the system is old, then you might well have a problem called "kettling", which means you'll need to get the whole system jet-flushed. However, try bleeding the radiators first, as sometimes a gurgling sound is

" careful with that drill, girl "

just air chugging around the pipes. If this doesn't work you might need to add some noise-inhibiting chemical to the system. Stop up the ballcock in the expansion tank and drain down until the tank is nearly empty (*see* p122–3). Try not to let the level go below the pipe where the water flows out – keep it airtight. Pour the chemical into the expansion tank and drain down a bit more so that it goes down into the pipes. Release the ballcock and let the tank refill as normal. After a few hours, bleed the radiators, just in case you've let air into the system.

A tapping sound from under the floorboards usually means that the pipes are knocking against something as they expand and contract, and you might need to clamp them down. "Careful with that drill, girl", says the voice of damp experience.

quick
budget
fixes

for the kitchen

Replacing a dodgy old kitchen is expensive, time-consuming, and seriously disruptive to a girl's life. In your heart of hearts you know if it needs to be done, but perhaps you can put up with the existing one while you are saving up.

If not, then a purely cosmetic facelift will cheer up any kitchen. This is especially useful for helping to sell a house, because the kitchen and bathroom are such important players in the house-selling game.

There are quite a lot of things you can do to liven up the kitchen, and most of them are relatively quick. I offer up a prayer that you don't pop round to visit me for a while – I've only done the first three things so far, and my old kitchen should be in a museum by now!

changing socket covers

The plug socket and light switch covers can be brought up to date with nicer ones. They are standard sizes so you can

" a purely cosmetic facelift

choose almost anything from the range. Be sure to switch off the whole house completely and follow the wiring diagrams on the pack. Just to be on the safe side, make a drawing of the old wiring before you start, in case you need to put it back on. And if you're not confident, call in a professional.

A word about metal switches with an earth wire: you will find that the earth is connected to the back of the switch box in or against the wall. And that there is a clearly marked "home" for the earth on the pattress (that's the posh name for a switch or socket cover – the visible bit). You must connect an earth "flyer" from the one in the back box to the home on the pattress. Just join one end of an extra bit in the screw with the old one and the other end in the pattress earth connection. About 15cm (6 in) should be enough.

A safety note for you: take extra care when screwing the cover back on so that you don't trap any wires or cut through them with the screws.

will cheer up any kitchen"

re-painting cupboards

Aha, the hand-painted look is in fashion these days. What a relief for those of us with tired old cupboards or dark and gloomy wood.

- You need to prime carefully so that the cupboards will accept the new paint and it will dry evenly.

- Next apply a coat of thinned, oil-based eggshell paint, about the consistency of single cream. Your brush strokes will dry nice and flat if you thin the paint. Check for drips and runs about five minutes after painting each door. Paint the middle panel first and then the edges.

- Rub down lightly when it is dry, using very fine grade sandpaper. Then re-coat. Three coats are best, especially if it's a dramatic colour change.

- Buy the most expensive brush you can afford – one with pure, long bristles. Work slowly and carefully, and perhaps listen to gentle music to keep you a bit mellow – if you rush you'll make a complete hash of it. Painted hinges look really naff, so go round them with care and clean up any over-paints. Rub away any dribbles before each coat. The effect is fabulous. Go on, you'll be amazed at the difference it makes.

changing handles

Changing the handles on cupboards is a bit like changing the buttons on a boring jacket – it takes diddly-squat effort and is totally transforming.

Count the handles and measure them. Put the details in a notebook to keep in your handbag, so that when you next pass a good knob and handle supplier you are ready to buy.

To keep it simple, replace handles with handles of the same size and knobs with knobs. This saves you from having to fill old holes and drill new ones. Measure the distance between the screw holes on your existing handles. There are two standard sizes and you may have a mixture.

The thickness of your doors might have an effect on the length of the screws you need. Short ones will be supplied with the handles, but make a note of what you have now in case you need longer ones.

- **replace handles with handles of the same size, and knobs with knobs**

adding interest to doors

adding moulding

This is a sure-fire way of bringing a bit of interest to flat doors. In theory, you can buy sticky-back mouldings ready-made to just press into place. In reality they fall off, so be ready to re-glue them with some decent adhesive. Nice idea though.

making your own beading

Cutting your own beading is simple if you have a small saw and a mitre block. As you mark up the lengths to cut, mark all the way across the beading, not just a little dot on the side. Mitre cutting is really easy to get in the wrong direction once you have looked away from the join you are making. The full pencil line helps.

Never cut a load of pieces at once, and never use a cut piece to measure against. You lose a tiny bit of the beading as sawdust and your bits will gradually get smaller. Actually, this applies to all woodwork. If you are cutting in the wrong direction you could waste a lot of your beading. In general the cut is 45 degrees but you don't need to worry – a mitre block has cutting grooves already set for you to slot your saw into. Put beading on before painting and then use some of that much-loved caulk or mastic around the seams and joins.

other handy things

useful tips

All the little notes in the margins of my writing pad and some of the excited helpful comments from my girly mates have piled up. Some of them are difficult to categorize, but you might appreciate the following tips.

lighting

A whole book in itself really, but just making one or two simple changes can be magic for the atmosphere of a room. Lighting around the edges of a room from lamps sort of washes up the walls and across the ceiling. This can be much more harmonious than a centre ceiling light, and goes especially well with Cabernet Sauvignon and the odd candle.

power failures

Keep a couple of torches, some candles, and a lighter in the same place all the time so that you can be sure to lay your hands on a light source and won't have to grope around in the dark.

internet shopping

Not for the faint-hearted because delivery is so erratic. Good and bad stories abound. Mine lean toward the bad. Definitely avoid important items from big companies at busy times of year, such as the January sales. Make sure you know the delivery date before paying. They take your money and then tell you it's going to be five weeks – believe me, that radiator never arrived. My blood boils just writing this. Enough said?

getting it delivered

Life is too short for waiting in at home for an unreliable delivery, but sometimes we just have to do it. When you find a reliable supplier, stick with them. They are worth their weight in chocolate profiteroles.

Try to fill a day at home with all of those other waiting-in jobs, like the washing-machine man or the guy coming to quote for your fence. Catch up on paperwork and phone calls.

If you can book the car in for a service on the same day then you get that done at a time when you can't be out driving anyway, and you'll get loads done while you are imprisoned in your house.

height issues

A glimpse of the blindingly obvious perhaps, but if you are tall, remember the height of your visitors when setting that mirror above the sink!

"of course you could always

If you are short then you might not be able to see that the third shelf down needs painting (or dusting), but everyone else will. Check your finish from the bottom steps of your ladder.

> ● **paint the top of any doors and frames near to the stairs**

Get down on the floor where you will someday fall asleep with a book over your nose. Did you miss the underside of the windowsill or the skirting under the radiator?

Do paint the top of doors and frames near to the stairs. You will see them as you come downstairs. Often you will be the first person ever to paint them, and it feels good to finish nicely.

oh, while you're down there ...

When you find yourself scrabbling under the floorboards for pipes or cables, or taking the bath panel off for something specific, have a look at the rest of it. Tidy up baggy cables while the floorboards are up, and shove the nozzle of the vacuum cleaner in as far as you can get. Wrap pipes to keep them separate and reduce noises, and pop some insulation into the section you have exposed some access to. These

"pop round and tell your Mum"

are the sorts of job that you might need to do one day, so it's worth paying some attention to them while you have the floorboards up so that you can avoid having to open them up again in the future.

phone your dad

Some Dads are just so full of out-of-date DIY blarney that you can be sure of a good laugh at their suggestions. However, some really know what they're doing and may even get straight in the car and come and help you out (result for you if you have a Dad like that). I phone my Dad after I've done something. He gets all proud of me and doesn't have to go through the worrying stage as I do it. "Dad, I've just put six halogen downlighters in the bedroom ceiling, on a dimmer switch"… Loud, worried spluttering sounds in my ear. Love it.

Of course you could always pop round and tell your Mum. They have this way of making everything so understated don't they? "That's nice darling. Would you like a cup of tea?"

acknowledgments

Thank you to my support mechanism:

Paul Jay for giving me a hug and the odd compliment, even at times when I don't look much like a lady, and for still doubting the combination of me and power tools.

Emily Anderson and Anna Sanderson for such a fun opportunity.

Yadzia Williams for the wild illustrations. I love them.

Joe and Joanna Barclay, because I wrote most of this in blissful solitude in the warmth of your Aga.

Eric Took, my electrical tutor, for helping electricity to make sense.